THE SARCASTIC BIG BOOK (SECOND EDITION)

The Story of How Thousands of Well-Intentioned Men and Women Have Totally Screwed Up the Original Message

Clay F

HJF Publishing

TABLE OF CONTENTS

- *Forward to the First Edition*
- *Forward to the Second Edition*
- *Some Doctor's Opinion*
- Chapter 1: A Co-Founder's Wordy Story
- Chapter 2: Is There a Solution?
- Chapter 3: More About our Endless Problems
- Chapter 4: We Are the Highest Power
- Chapter 5: Doing the Deal
- Chapter 6: Into Thinking
- Chapter 7: Working on Others
- Chapter 8: To Sex Partners
- Chapter 9: In Rehab Afterward
- Chapter 10: A Vision Askew
- *Afterward*
- *The No Steps Prayer*

CONTENTS

Title Page
Table of Contents
Preface
Forward to the First Edition   1
Forward to the Second Edition   2
Some Doctor's Opinion   4
Chapter 1   5
Chapter 2   7
Chapter 3   11
Chapter 4   15
Chapter 5   18
Chapter 6   24
Chapter 7   33
Chapter 8   38
Chapter 9   43
Chapter 10   47
Afterward   51
The No Steps Prayer   53
Books By This Author   55

PREFACE

One morning years ago, I had arrived early to a local 12-Step meeting hall. Just outside stood a man, by himself, trembling terribly.

"You alright?", I asked.

"No," he told me. "I'm not alright at all. I want to drink so bad right now."

I stood with him awhile, offering empathy and asking questions. He said he was an alcoholic, and that he had known it for years. Shaking, he stared at the pavement, as if gazing only at the horrendous reality of his inner predicament - that alcoholic hell. He could hardly speak. I asked him about the 12 Steps.

"Oh, my sponsor won't let me start the steps for thirty days."

I never saw him again.

I have had countless interactions like this, all of which I find heartbreaking. Just imagine where we might be had Bill told Bob to wait thirty days before starting the steps. Moreover, and strange as it is to say, much of what is commonly shared in meetings completely opposes the original text ("This is a selfish program"; "I can never trust my thinking"; "We are forever recovering", e.g.). One could easily argue that, in the big picture, all this confusion is just fine; many still get well in spite of it. I see that, believe me. Yet I have daily interactions with people whose struggling is, I think, completely avoidable, and perhaps due to the fact they've received a twisted message. And it is because of hundreds of such encounters that I decided to write this book.

My incredible experience in recovery, as it relates to the Steps, has been the result of the *very opposite of everything you are about to read*. Suffice it to say, I disagree with every word. Saddest, however, is that *I have not made any of this up*. Sometimes it sounds downright shocking, but I've taken no liberties. Every single thing in here has been told to me in various ways, *literally thousands of times*.

I have not rewritten the Big Book - but based on everything I hear, many others have. So I just wanted to see what that message would look like were it actually written down.

FORWARD TO THE FIRST EDITION

We are a diminishing group of men and women whose amazing experience actually resembles the incredible experience described in the original "Big Book." To show other alcoholics, through the heavy use of sarcasm, *precisely how far away from that message we have strayed* is the main purpose of this book. For them, we hope these pages will effectively point out the absolute ridiculousness of much of what is commonly spoken, taught, and accepted in the world of recovery today, thus inspiring a reevaluation of the actual "Big Book".

What is written here may be found offensive to some. And maybe it should be - because these pages contain nothing but a sadly accurate description of exactly what has been constantly reflected back to its author for several decades.

FORWARD TO THE SECOND EDITION

Since the first printing of this book roughly one year ago, remarkable things have happened. The message in this book has clearly resonated with people from around the world. In fact, at the time of this writing, there are weekly meetings that use *The Sarcastic Big Book* as a basis for discussion - two in the United States, and one in Russia. Thrilling to me is that the people who started these groups understand the point of *The Sarcastic Big Book*.

This edition brings two brand new chapters: "To Sex Partners", and "In Rehab Afterward." Moreover, its original chapters are now longer, and some things have been slightly re-written.

On the one hand, the fact that this book contains a message relatable to so many recovery communities is of no surprise, as I have lived all over the United States and have heard similar things everywhere I've been. On the other hand, the fact that this book contains a universal message continues to amaze me. And I am thrilled by the amount of laughter and levity it's brought to the lives of thousands. I've received so many of the most wonderful and uplifting messages and e-mails since its initial publication, thanking me for writing this book. More than anything though, is that this parody, written from love, contains an inverted message that has already proven to be helpful beyond that of which I'd ever dreamed.

SOME DOCTOR'S OPINION

Many years ago, when horses and buggies roamed the streets, some brilliant doctor wrote a bunch of incredible insight, based on his personal experience with helping thousands of drug addicts and alcoholics, that you can basically disregard. Nevermind that science finally caught up with his findings in the 2010's. It's just a bunch of boring crap your sponsor may ask you to read. Just tell him or her that you've read it, that you understand now, and that you're good to go.

Besides, if you are in a treatment center, it is likely you will be asked to *go against just about everything he wrote, anyway* - you might see a therapist because you need to understand *why* you are an alcoholic; you may be told to avoid "triggers", that you just need to keep busy, that your brain is damaged beyond repair, etc.... So don't bother with this stuff some doctor wrote back when movies were made using black and white film.

Okay, you've read it! Go tell your sponsor! You're good to go!

CHAPTER 1
A CO-FOUNDER'S WORDY STORY

Blah blah alcohol blah blah blah blah blah blah blah blah blah blah blah blah blah blah blah blah blah blah blah blah blah alcohol blah blah blah blah blah blah blah blah blah blah blah blah blah blah blah blah blah blah blah blah blah blah blah blah blah blah blah blah blah blah blah blah alcohol blah blah blah blah blah blah blah blah blah blah blah.

Blah blah blah blah blah blah blah blah blah blah blah blah blah blah blah blah blah blah blah blah blah blah blah blah blah blah blah blah blah blah blah blah blah blah blah blah blah blah blah blah blah blah blah blah blah blah blah blah blah blah blah blah blah blah blah blah blah blah blah blah blah blah blah blah blah blah blah blah blah blah blah blah blah blah blah blah blah blah blah blah blah blah blah blah blah blah blah blah blah blah blah blah blah blah blah blah

blah blah blah blah blah blah blah blah blah blah blah blah blah blah blah blah blah blah blah.

   Blah blah blah blah blah blah blah blah blah blah blah blah blah blah blah blah blah blah blah blah blah blah blah blah blah blah blah blah blah blah blah blah blah blah blah alcohol blah blah blah blah blah blah blah blah blah blah blah blah blah blah blah blah blah blah blah blah blah blah blah alcohol blah blah blah blah blah blah blah blah blah blah blah blah blah blah blah blah blah blah blah blah blah blah blah blah blah blah blah blah blah blah blah blah blah blah blah alcohol blah blah blah blah blah blah blah blah blah blah blah blah blah. Blah blah blah blah blah blah blah blah blah blah blah blah blah blah blah blah blah blah blah blah blah blah blah blah blah blah blah blah blah blah blah blah blah blah blah blah blah blah blah blah blah blah blah blah blah blah blah blah blah blah blah blah. Blah blah blah bathtub gin. Blah blah blah blah. Blah blah blah blah blah blah blah blah blah.

CHAPTER 2
IS THERE A SOLUTION?

We know thousands of men and women who were once just as hopeless as the co-founder. Many of them now spend months or years going in and out of treatment centers and sober livings.

Much of this world is represented, and we are people who would not normally interact with one another. Yet we all decided to do something about our drinking. Either because we really wanted to, or because someone else was making us. Either way, we are all lumped together here now.

Is there a solution? Almost none of us enjoyed the thought of having to do this for the rest of our lives, but the fact is, we are bound together by a solution we call *basically just going to meetings*. Many attend daily. Some of us are so situated that we are able to attend multiple meetings a day. More fortunate still are those of us who are in a position where, due to the enabling nature of either family, insurance companies, or both, we are able to attend countless meetings each week without even having to drive ourselves there.

Some of you are thinking, "Just go to meetings? Really? That's it?" Well, the answer is...yes. We understand your skepticism. It often appears there should be more to it. After all, few actually stay very long, and many of those who do still seem quite restless and irritable. But it isn't so bad. I mean, we're hanging in there. Besides, we have some commonplace sayings that frequently cheer us up: "Life is in session." "It is what it is." "It's just life on life's terms." "Everyone gets their turn in the barrel" is another comforting thing you'll hear often.

While such phrases don't always do the trick, they do tend to lighten our load sometimes. Doubtless some will still ask, "But just exactly how are these meetings going to keep me sober?" Here's how: we need to be reminded of how terrible it is to drink and use drugs. Seeing struggling newcomers on a regular basis really drives this home for us. "Whew," we can say to ourselves, "Sure glad that ain't me." Sure, this may seem self-centered, but keep in mind, even after years of abstinence, everything should still be all about us.

While this alone is enough to permanently strengthen the resolve of many in our crowd, there are other reasons to go, as well. Meetings are a great place to judge people. And because of something called the Traditions, attacking a meeting is not unlike punching a blindfolded child from behind. It cannot defend itself or fight back. So we take comfort in that, and, momentarily, lift ourselves up a little simply by looking down at others in the room trying to better themselves. Besides, it is smart to go somewhere in order to receive free help, reject that help, and then criticize all of it. That just makes perfect sense.

Another reason we keep going to meetings is to please our sponsors. We have mumblings on our coins about being true to yourself, but never forget that the program is all about pleasing other people. It is frustrating when someone is unhappy with us, so we avoid this at all costs - no matter the price to our heart and soul.

But not everyone who decides to attend meetings will do so for the reasons mentioned. For instance, many still go year after year just so they can hear themselves talk as much as they like. Sensing that a meeting can be a stage of sorts, some go so far as to carefully prepare what they are going to share, peppering their musings with either slick sayings that are sure to get collective sighs, or jokes that have proven in the past to get rousing guffaws. This feels freakin' good! And, again, our feeling good is what it's always going to be about.

Not all of us are extroverted. Some have been sober for years but feel they have nothing to verbally contribute to the group. That's fine. *That we are physically sitting there is the main thing.* So whether we decide to share, play on our phone, or simply prop our ass in a corner like a house plant, it does not matter. That our body is in the room means we are doing more than enough.

There are banners with some numbered shit hanging on the walls of practically every meeting, but don't pay too much attention to that stuff. The point is that, as alcoholics, we are going to be all fucked up for the rest of our lives. So temporarily feeling a little better about ourselves, by simply showing up, is the best we can do. Anything more than this should not be expected.

Sometimes you'll hear people in meetings talk about spiritual-sounding stuff. Don't freak out. People say all kinds of things. Just focus on suiting up and showing up at the meetings. We all know that once money or sex come into the picture, all that spiritual crap flies right out the window, anyway. Therefore, once you get around to looking for someone to help you on this journey, focus on the important stuff - their car, their clothes, that kind of shit.

Since we've always been excellent liars, living a double life in the rooms should come naturally. "I'm doing great," is one of our most popular superficial mantras. How we seem to be doing to others will always matter more than how we are actually doing. And if you're from a home where real feelings were never expressed anyway, this will be a breeze. You can slide right into the kind of dysfunction you already find to be a comfort of sorts.

After all, life is in session. It is what it is.

CHAPTER 3
MORE ABOUT OUR ENDLESS PROBLEMS

Most of us have been unwilling to admit that we have more shortcomings than normal folk. This sounds ridiculous, but for the sake of argument, we'll just pretend it's true. There is nothing we can really do about our defects except write, think, and talk about them incessantly for the rest of our lives. If we don't do this, we will surely drink again. Makes sense, right? I mean, the solution is to focus on the problem. For example, if a man has poor eyesight, he must learn about *why* he can't see - and then talk about it, dwell upon it, write about it - and that's basically the same thing for him as wearing glasses. In fact, discussing our problems into the ground is another reason we continue going to meetings long after we have "done the work." Further on, we shall describe that work in detail.

We learned that we had to fully concede to our innermost selves that we were stuck being selfish scamps. This is the first step in our recovery. The delusion that we could gradually become less selfish has to be smashed. Life is always going be a struggle. The desire to get your own way will seldom even diminish, let alone vanish. You are just too fucked up to authentically care about another human being. Sure, you'll have moments, but that's it. We do not entertain the notion that empathy and compassion can be endlessly expanded. The idea that one can *actually* lose interest in selfish things is a pipedream; poetry for the foolish simpleton.

We are like an endless amount of gender identities who have lost their legs. In fact, in many cases, we are were never even born *with* legs! Either way, we never grow new ones. What this means is we are stuck with a spiritual malady so unique and perverse that even an act of providence can only scratch its surface. Heaven knows we have tried hard enough and long enough to relate to "normal" people, on at least some level. But we cannot!

No one has to, but should you make an attempt at the actual steps, don't go overboard. Some of us made the mistake of setting our standards for spiritual growth high, but learned that this was just an expectation. And expectations will only lead to resentments. And resentments will lead us right back to drinking. So don't expect anything. Prepare yourself for a very so-so experience. You are not alone!

Since living this way will seldom be that comfortable, some of us found it necessary to seek constant direction from others in the fellowship. Aside from being people with whom we can talk about our own endless process of defining who we are, they will be by our side so they can let us know when we can go the bathroom, where we can work, who we can fuck, and so on. Many are glad to help. Highly competent psychiatrists who have dealt with us have found it sometimes impossible to give us any real aid. Strangely enough, wives, husbands, parents, and friends haven't been able to do much with us, either.

But the person with a thinking problem who has found this solution, and who is still pretty miserable himself, can generally win the confidence of another alcoholic in a few months. Until such an understanding is reached, little can actually happen.

That the person making the approach is still having the same difficulties, that other people tell you that this person knows what they're talking about, that they literally shout at the new prospect in a way that is totally Holier Than Thou, that it is made quite clear there are axes to grind, people to please, and lectures to be endured. That there are motives other than a sincere desire to be helpful - these are the conditions we have found most common. After such an approach, many follow along dutifully for months, and sometimes years.

Some of our readers may still believe that they can achieve what we have accomplished without relying on other people for constant guidance. Let us make an illustration.

Fred is a partner at a large automobile dealership. He has a charming wife and two young children. He has found a Higher Power, and has maintained his sobriety for over fifteen years. He attends roughly three meetings a week. He sponsors other men, and participates in functions regularly hosted by his local fellowship. Yet he does not check in with another alcoholic each and every morning. Here is the fellow who has really been tripping you out, especially in the way he declares that he is doing just fine. One day, before a meeting, some members of our crowd confronted him. We told him we didn't think he was doing it right. In fact, we gave him an earful, leaving him with plenty to think about.

We heard no more from Fred for awhile. When we finally did see him again, he seemed standoffish and mildly irritated by our presence. After the meeting, we cornered him before he was able to leave, asking him where the fuck he'd been for the past few months. And boy, did he tell us.

"I listened to what you folks had to say. But I gotta be honest, I really don't understand where you get off trying to tell everyone else what they need to do. I have a God of my understanding, and my life is really good. I pray all the time. I do not feel I am in danger of drinking, and, frankly, I attend meetings in a different part of town now, kinda because of you. But thanks, as always, for your opinion."

While it may be true that Fred doesn't feel he needs to change anything, feelings aren't facts. We know that his sobriety is on thin ice. And if we were in his position, we would feel like we were about to be picked off or something. But if Fred can't follow direction, that's on him. We know that a Higher Power alone won't keep us from drinking. Our defense must come from another person.

CHAPTER 4
WE ARE THE HIGHEST POWER

*I*n the preceding chapters you have learned something about alcoholism as it is commonly explained nowadays. We hope we have made clear today's distinction between the alcoholic and the non-alcoholic. If you are extremely selfish, or you never felt like you fit in, or you have little to no attention span, you are probably alcoholic. If that be the case, you may be suffering from something for which there appears to be no real solution because, after all, we are powerless over everything - our decisions, our behavior, how we respond to others and to the events in our lives. There's nothing for us to do except sit back and passively just let whatever happens happen.

Lack of power, that was our dilemma. We had to find a power by which we could live, and that power is called a *sponsor*. However, completely relying on another person is kind of embarrassing, so we will want to at least pretend we are trying to do more. And that means we are going to talk to you about God.

To one who feels he is atheist or agnostic, the subject of God brings up fear. Fear that we will need to start having to take the God idea really seriously. But don't worry. While it is true that there are some in our fellowship who actually do take God seriously, trusting and relying upon Him completely, some of us strictly *talk about relying upon God*, but basically keep doing whatever the hell we want. We pray alright, but the moment we open our eyes, we get right down to the business of playing God. Especially when money is involved. That's just a seperate thing. We'll mention God a lot, but there's stuff we'll for sure have to try and control. Including people - both in and out of the rooms. Having been sober awhile, not only do we know what's best for us, we know what's best for everyone else now. Sure, we might tell you to "pray about it", but that will seem a faint footnote by the time you are done sifting through the heaps of personal advice we'll give you. We have been there, done that. We freely admit that we do not trust our own thinking, but we'll be asking you to trust us when it comes to what you should be doing in *your* life. The point to all this is that we will tell you what to do, so don't work yourself into a lather about any of the spiritual stuff. Plenty of us found we have not had to take the God idea *that* seriously.

We only had to ask ourselves one question. "Do I now believe, or am I willing to believe, that I can throw the word 'God' around with the best of 'em?"

As soon as a man can say that he does believe, or is willing to believe, we emphatically assure him that he is good to go. It has been repeatedly proven among us that this is more than enough to get by. *The actual application of spiritual principles is hard.* We understand that things won't always go our way, and that, in general, we need to become more accepting of stuff. But sometimes people totally wrong us. Seriously! They do. *They* are the ones who are wrong! Honestly! In cases like these, there is no need to look for a spiritual solution. I mean, it is what it is.

This was great news for us, for we had assumed we had to

start actually trying to practice spiritual principles in *all* our affairs. It was comforting to learn we could muddle through at a way easier level.

CHAPTER 5
DOING THE DEAL

Often have we seen a person fail who has thoroughly followed our path. Those who do not stay sober are people who cannot or will not completely give themselves to this simple program, usually men and women who are immediately thrown off by our totally confusing message. It's either that, or maybe they have jobs that are more demanding, relationships more complicated, and personal issues that are just too perplexing for us to understand. Their chances are below average. There are those too who have already *done* the steps (despite the fact this technically impossible; see definition of the word 'continued') and have still not been able to remain sober.

Our stories disclose in a general way how hardcore we used to be, and, briefly, how "it's all good" now. If you have decided you want what we have and are willing to *verbally express* that you will go to any lengths to get it - then you are ready to take these steps. At some of these we looked up from our phones and said, "Fuuuuuck that." We thought we could find an easier way, but we could not. And with all the earnestness at our command we beg of you to wait at least one year before you sponsor anyone. Some of us tried to be helpful to people right away, and were hollered at until we let go absolutely. Remember that we deal with alcohol, heroin, marijuana, oxycodone, methamphetamines - whatever - cunning, baffling, powerful! Without help it's too much for us. But there is one who has all power - that one is your sponsor - you should call him now!

Half measures availed us free room and board in sober livings. We stood at a fork in the road. We asked for our sponsor's protection with complete abandon.

Here are the steps we took, which are suggested as a program of recovery:
1) We wrote about our alcoholism in detail so we could strengthen our self-knowledge concerning our alcoholism
2) Came to believe that we would always be insane, that the original authors must have just chosen their words at random
3) Made a decision to go to ninety meetings in ninety days
4) Reluctantly followed some worksheet that confirmed we were pieces of shit
5) Admitted to God, to ourselves, and to another human being that we basically sucked, and would always be fucked up to some extent
6) Were entirely ready to have God remove any defects of character that we were not still quietly enjoying
7) Let someone else do the searching and fearless part of this process by supplying us with a list of our shortcomings
8) Made a list of persons we had harmed - the ones we pretty much knew had forgiven us already, anyway
9) Made direct amends to people from a list that was given to us by our sponsor, except when to do so would arouse an old flame or land us in jail

10) Continued to let others call us out whenever they caught us doing something we already knew was wrong

11) Sought through weights and medication to improve our conscious contact with God as we understood Him, praying only for people to do certain things, and for shit to go a certain way

12) Having "finished" the steps, we tried to get back into the things that truly mattered to us, and talked down to newcomers as often as possible

Many of us exclaimed, "But I'm an alcoholic and am therefore permanently defiant!" Do not be discouraged. Many of us haven't gotten too far past that, either. We are not saints. And the point is, we have to choose between being a saint or a selfish asshole. Or you can just say "progress not perfection" and keep basically doing whatever!

Our description of the alcoholic, the chapter about acceptance, and our personal adventures before and after make clear three ideas:

a) That we were alcoholic and could not manage our own lives

b) That no other human being could manage our lives, either

c) That a sponsor could try to, and would try to, if he were sought

Being convinced, *we were at Step Three*, which is that we decided to go to ninety meetings in ninety days. Just what do we mean by that, and just what do we do? We mean this: make a decision to attend ninety meetings during a span of ninety days, and then do that. However, by the time you're done attending ninety meetings, you'll basically want to peel your own face off. By that time, you'll need something else to do, for sure.

Therefore we next moved at a snail's pace through a personal inventory. *This was Step Four.* Since doing an inventory is designed to begin to remove whatever self-will has blocked you off from God, really take your sweet time with this one. Obviously there is no hurry. Because the sooner we did this, the sooner we would commence to take full responsibility for our lives. Blaming other people for our problems would make less and less sense, and eventually we might lose our whole victim mentality. We would begin to sense there to be no justifiable reason to complain about anything anymore. We would start thinking about ourselves less often, as it would become clearer and clearer that this world does not owe us a goddamn thing. Eventually, we'd actually want to be of service to others. *So do not rush this process.* Its completion spells the beginning of the end of your bullshit. Besides, we could remind ourselves, there are plenty of do-gooders already. This world has gotten along just fine without our contributing much of anything to anyone. Why start now simply because our very lives were saved?

Happily, we know of many ways to slow the inventory

process to a crawl. Acting confused is popular: "So, how many columns again?" Or, "Wait, do I write *everything*?" Getting all tangled up in the specificity of the form is a common one, too: "I think I have to re-write everything because I didn't do the columns very neatly." In fact, perfectionism is such an effective crutch that some members use it as an excuse which prevents them from ever finishing this step at all.

Whatever course you choose, the guiding principle is this: we have been promised tons of tomorrows in this life, so move like molasses. Besides, if you are anything like us, you've basically treated everyone wonderfully for years, anyway. So do not be hasty about putting your feet on any new soil.

Use working on your inventory as an opportunity to get more attention than usual. Moan to anyone who will listen that you feel terrible about how selfishly you've behaved, but don't be in a rush when it comes to actually changing anything about your behavior. Regarding your inventory, share in meetings in a way that implies that you are *really* sick - sicker than most. It's possible to drag this on for months, or even years. There are a couple paths you can take in order to achieve this. Option one: barely write at all. One or two names a day, if that. And only do that because then you're not technically lying when you tell people you're working on it. Make literally anything that comes along during your day more important than working on your inventory. And when you do finally crack open your notebook, barely lift a finger. Option two: write constantly. Make it so complex that even *you* don't understand what the fuck you're doing anymore. Write pages and pages about the harms *done to you,* and write about it in great detail so you are able to re-live it and get angry and sad. On the bright side, this route will be extremely effective in terms of keeping you from getting to the actual inventory - you know, *your* part. Drag the first two columns on and on and on and on.

But, if you happen to be a reader who actually wants to complete the fourth step in a timely manner, we suggest a worksheet of some kind, something you can easily download from the internet.

CHAPTER 6
INTO THINKING

Having made our personal inventory, what shall we do next? We have put off moving forward in every way we could. We have regularly attended meetings for months. We have pretended we were confused and in need of further clarification. We have asked multiple people in the fellowship the same questions, using their conflicting answers as another reason to stall. We have switched sponsors. We have faked being sick. We have worked on it during meetings, thus paying little attention to either the inventory or the meeting itself. But there are no two ways about it - we have somehow wound up with an inventory we can call finished.

Now it is time to read it aloud to another human being, which, when we are finished, will mean we have completed *Step Five* in the program suggested. Some of us found the idea of having such an intimate conversation difficult. But don't worry. If you have a good sponsor, they will do most of the talking. Some sponsors will look at this as an opportunity to really dig into another person without seeming like they are mean. If they do talk down to you, they'll probably tell you it's for your own good. You jotted down shit in a notebook for months. That was hard. Now let your sponsor do the digging and the searching. They should be the one who find your defects of character. Why should you have to do it? Allow them to let you know how fucked up you are. Take what they may say at face value, no matter the dissonance it causes.

Perhaps you have suffered from a legitimately traumatic experience in the past. While most sponsors are not qualified to navigate such waters, many will be happy to pretend that they can. Having never received the formal education of an actual therapist or psychiatrist, some spot this as an opportunity, and will jump at the chance to momentarily play the part.

Once we have completed this step, we feel more confused than ever. On the one hand, we are angry about what was said to us. On the other hand, we have been told for months now that our own brains are literally useless. This is a lot to sort through. We bring this disillusionment into meetings, sharing about how sick we feel after finishing the fifth step. After a while, so many people will tell us they felt the same way that we can begin to convince ourselves this is normal.

When we get around to it, we find a place where we can be quiet for an hour. Taking this book down from our shelf we turn to the page which contains the twelve steps, carefully reviewing the first five of them. Have we been taking this crap seriously? The answer doesn't really matter. Either way, let's look at *Step Six*.

Your sponsor already outlined your flaws for you. Are you now willing to be consumed with those defects, all day, every day? Are you ready to doubt every thought you have, and question every move that you make? Are you willing to analyze yourself to the point where you are not at all present for anyone around you?

When ready, we said something like this. *My creator, please help me remember that my sponsor is smarter than my own conscience.* We have then completed *Step Seven*.

Next, we kicked back for months.

Eventually, the malaise brought about by our flickering attendance at meetings drove us to pick up our pens yet again, this time, to make a list of persons we had harmed by our conduct. *This was Step Eight.* Do not hurt yourself trying to do this one - let your sponsor do it for you. They will tell you which amends are valid and which ones are trash. Remember that amends are unrelated to what you feel in your own heart; this is about following sponsor direction.

So even though our sponsors do not trust their own thinking when it comes to their own lives, we completely trust their thinking when it comes to ours, allowing them to carefully map out the path our soul needs to take in *Step Nine*. And we still may have no desire to apologize to anyone, but don't worry. Most of us were told to only make amends to about a half dozen people.

Since at this point everything should still be about us, this step should be viewed as something that we simply need to get out of the way. It's not about whether or not these people actually deserve an amends. It's about us. Therefore, feel free to make this step as mechanical as possible. People might feel quietly uneasy about your communicating with them using notecards or a script. They may prefer that you speak to them from the heart instead. Fuck that. Remember, it's really not about their experience. It's about ours.

Some of us were not too keen on the idea of telling people we had ill feelings about them, especially if such information was going to be brand-new news to them. We did it anyway, dropping emotional bombs on those of whom never knew we hated their guts. This hurt their feelings, but so what. We felt better afterwards, and that was all that mattered.

Most alcoholics owe money.
And?

I mean, most of us were nowhere near taking the financial part of this step too seriously. Some of us still chuckle at the notion that, in the 1930's, sober alcoholics regularly confronted that kind of thing head on.

Concerning amends needing to be made to those with whom we've had intimate relations, fuck it. We were too sick in the head to try and approach any ex-boyfriends, ex-girlfriends, ex-lovers, or ex-spouses. Even if we tried, we would only stir up old hurts and feelings again. It is better to just try to pretend those relationships never happened. They may be hurting badly, but there is really nothing we can do. Oh well. Just hope you don't run into them anywhere. If you do, look the other way or find the nearest exit. Alcoholics are good at doing that. Besides, the very idea of going to them with crystal clear, spiritually sound motives is ridiculous, anyway. We are incapable of such an errand. We might get super turned on when we saw them, and, quickly jumping back in bed together, would only make things worse than they were in the first place.

Usually your ex is seeing someone else by now. Get it out of your head that any current partner your ex may have is capable of grasping the idea of an honest amends. Their new mate will be all messed up by the sheer sound of your name. They will be convinced that you have only reached out so that you can drudge up old feelings or fuck their wife or husband again.

There are a couple things we can do at home. Our spouses, parents, and siblings have put up with our crap for years, but it's not like we owe them the world or anything. They're not saints, either. Nonetheless, when it's convenient for us, we sit down with the family and, frankly, remind them that at least we're not drinking. Sometimes we tell them we will try to do better in general. But this is a two-way street. They'd better start owning up to some of their shit, too. For if they do not start behaving better, let them know we are likely to drink again. If their bad conduct continues, avoid them. Sometimes this is not possible, due to various gatherings we feel obligated to attend. This is one of the reasons some communities host marathon meetings during the holidays. There you'll find a forum where you can complain about your still-annoying family members year after year after year after year.

If we have been painstaking about this, we will be kinda bummed that we're only a little more than halfway through. We are going to start missing our old "freedom" and our old "happiness." We will try to forget the past, but find we cannot slam the door on it. We may hear about serenity, but still not know peace. No matter how far along we've come, we won't really be sure we can help anyone. That feeling of uselessness and self-pity may reappear. Our self-esteem may slip away. Our old attitude and outlook upon life might remain. We'll avoid people, and we will work a ton so we don't face economic insecurity. How we're told to handle situations will sometimes baffle us. We will suddenly realize that people are doing things for us that we should probably be doing for ourselves.

Does any of this sound good at all? These things are happening all around us - sometimes quickly, sometimes slowly. And they will always happen if we allow it.

This thought brings us to *Step Ten*, which suggests we continue to basically do whatever we want and let other people call us out on stuff. We started doing this long before we got sober. Now we just stick with it. Continue to listen for that voice inside telling you that you are doing something wrong. When it crops up, talk to other people who are doing similar things. When others are doing the same shit, it is way easier to rationalize our behavior.

And we continue fighting everyone and everything - including alcohol. For by this time we have been repeatedly told we will always be insane, that the original second step was not specific to the thought preceding the first drink. Concerning the thought of drinking, however... it comes and goes, and is dependent on outside circumstances. If we are on shaky ground, we call another alcoholic and talk about ourselves. We do our best to avoid temptation. When in serious danger of relapse, we call our sponsor, even if we sponsor others. If we are unable to reach our sponsor, we run to the nearest meeting. This is what we do. This should be the plan for the rest of our sobriety.

Step Eleven suggests that we exercise, take steroids, and pray for things in our life to go a certain way. The first part of this step is simple. Science has taught us all kinds of awesome stuff about endorphins. Get in excellent physical shape. Sometimes a member is slow to realize that if you are doing this shit properly meeting halls should be viewed as, basically, health clubs. Gym memberships are not that expensive. Besides, think about how much money you used to blow on booze and heroin. Forking out a little extra cash for the use of treadmills, or steroids, is nothing.

Little has been said about receiving guidance through prayer and meditation. But we feel we should bring it up briefly. If one continues to try to play God, prayer and meditation will only bring faint results anyway. And since trying to play God, by remaining attached to how *we* believe life should go, both for ourselves and for others, is the biggest portion of this step, that's about all we'll say about prayer and meditation.

Moving on.

When we retire at night, we gloss over the events of our day. Did we treat people in the program better than we treated those with whom we live? Were we careful to give lots of unsolicited advice? Did we do most of the talking during interactions, thus ensuring we were both aggravating others, as well as learning nothing new? Did we try to manage what others thought about us? About other people? Did we nessle our nose into the business of our fellows, justifying it because our motives were so good? Was most of our inner dialog about money? Did we tell ourselves that our fears were simply appropriate concerns? Did we complain as much as we could to anyone within earshot? If we could honestly say yes, then perfect. *None of this should ever change.*

Upon awakening we think about precisely how the day needs to unfold. We contemplate how much happier we'd be if people would only do shit a certain way. We remind ourselves it's okay to boss people around, since our motives are good. We think fast and talk fast, knowing that a quick mind is usually very healthy. We rush through the day, making sure everything around us is in perfect order. If things fall apart, we bark orders at those responsible for ruining our plan. As alcoholics, we repeatedly tell ourselves we will be extremely selfish and self-centered forever. This does two things. First, it keeps us from having to grow much. And second, it excuses a whole bunch of junk.

We may have to interact with people who are not alcoholic. "Normies" don't have fears or worries or resentments; non-alcoholics feel great all the time. They have no spiritual battles whatsoever. They don't have insecurities. They just automatically "get" life and always do the right thing with no effort. So keep yourself separate from them. *You have nothing in common.*

As we go through the day, we pause when someone pisses us off, and hold in our real feelings. *Pray for them, but then avoid them as much as humanly possible.* If circumstances warrant, complain about them to others. Once you've gotten it off your chest, say, "It's all *good*" or "Love and Tolerance" out loud. Then sweep your anger under a rug and move on.

It doesn't really work - but life is in session.

Now there is much more action to take, which is perfect because, by now, we are likely driving our family members almost as crazy as they are driving us. We need a place where we can try to run the show with a certain amount of impunity. The next chapter is entirely devoted to talking down to other alcoholics!

CHAPTER 7
WORKING ON OTHERS

Our experience shows that nothing will so much guarantee us a place in society as sponsoring other people in the fellowship. This is our *Twelfth Suggestion*. Carry this message to them! You alone can keep them sober. You can take over their decision-making, both personal and professional. Remember they are very sick. They will need you until they are lowered into the earth.

Life will take on a brand new meaning. To have people *finally fucking listen to you*. To have a host of followers around you. To witness them reluctantly adhering to your advice. To see fear in their eyes when you tell them that you need to talk to them. This is an experience you must not miss. Working on others is one of the best parts of our lives.

In olden times, alcoholics had to do a lot of footwork to find newcomers. Not anymore. There are thousands of meetings throughout the world. All you have to do is show up at any one of them and announce you have the sobriety they want. Newer members are often vulnerable, and, not being sure of how it all works, will sometimes approach you afterwards. If not, hunt them down and force yourself upon them until they feel trapped.

Don't waste time getting to know anything about them. Tell them right away they had better do it your way, or they might drink again. Make it clear from day one that it's your way or the highway. If they resist you, threaten them. Say things like, "Do whatever you want. Look where *that*'s gotten you." Intimidate the shit out of them. Many, thinking this is normal, will eventually go along willingly.

Next, test them. Tell them that you don't believe they are sincere, that you'll need proof. Ask them to call you every day for a month. If they do this, then you can start giving them the time of day. Why should you be bothered with someone in need of immediate attention and support? You are busy. You *have* your business back already. You're an important person again. Perhaps you are a homeowner who is married with kids. Money doesn't grow on trees, and you work for a living. Such a lifestyle can take up a lot of time, so don't waste too much of yours now just because someone else is drowning.

If your prospect does call you every day, never honor such a person by picking up the phone every time. This is about testing their resolve, and has nothing to do with forming a genuine human connection. If they miss calling you once, fuck them. They are not serious about getting sober. There can be no other explanation. Let whatever will happen to them happen. Tell your friends in recovery about the new person being unable to follow your simple instruction. Get them to talk some shit of their own.

Let's say that, every day for thirty days, your prospect actually called you and has somehow white-knuckled abstinence. You are now fairly sure they mean business. Lend them this book and tell them to read specific parts of it all on their own. If they propose that you meet with them in person, so you can go over it together, tell them they are already being defiant and deride them for suggesting it. Remind them they are not to trust themselves, only you. Tell them over and over again that their best thinking got them here - suggest they not use their own brain for anything at all.

If they have carefully followed your instructions, agree to meet with them once a week. Make them feel they are in a class of some kind, driving it home that you are their teacher, and the steps are assignments. If they bring up any ideas given to them by others in the fellowship, insist they listen to you and you alone; if they are going to start trying to absorb any wisdom from other people, tell them they're only allowed to follow your direction and threaten to drop them.

Help them strengthen their self-knowledge concerning drinking. If you have them write about it, also have them jot down all the ways they are totally fucked up unrelated to alcohol. Muddy the waters further by telling them they will never recover or be restored to sanity. Next, grade their work as if it were a school paper. "This is wrong," tell them, "go back and do it again." Make it plain that your feelings about their effort, their progress, or lack thereof, is what is important here. It is tremendously helpful when you repeat this sentiment for months, because it keeps their attention focused on the plot of recovery.

Once you are finally satisfied with the work they have turned in, robotically guide them through the remaining steps in the way that was outlined in the previous chapter. Throughout this process, continuously discourage them from deciding anything for themselves, whether they feel a connection to a higher power or not. Constantly remind them they will always be insane, that the original second step was made up of arbitrary words, and not meant to mean anything specific to alcohol.

Do not, at any point, bring up the Traditions. There's just too much to get into. If they show interest, say something vague about the Traditions applying only to the group, and not to the individual, and then change the subject. With your permission, someone else can go over that stuff with them later on.

If your prospect relapses, but returns to meetings, make him feel weird about it. Look at him with disappointment or don't look at him at all. If he summons the courage to speak to you, tell him he fucked up, plain and simple. Remind the new man how bad he is at taking direction. It should not matter if he storms out and leaves the rooms forever. It is what it is. Some will quickly return, trying all the harder to please you. Others may come crawling back later.

Carry your sobriety around like a shiny trophy you earned all on your own. You're on top again, so shove this fact in people's faces whenever it's possible. If anyone criticises you for some reason, run from the idea that you might be wrong about something. If you don't do this, newer members may think you're not working a good program and will be less likely to listen to what you say.

While drinking we withdrew from most circles. Now we have one. But be careful not to dedicate your whole life to it. There are mortgages to pay, mouths to feed, and there is money to be made. You have been given a second chance in life. Don't throw it away now by spending too much of your time bending over backwards for people who don't have their own shit together yet.

> *We fight to get our own way!*
> *We have to!*
> *No one's gonna do it for us!*

CHAPTER 8
TO SEX PARTNERS

Until this chapter, this book has only addressed the alcoholic. But usually, the alcoholic, whose life is spinning wildly out of control, is having sex with at least one person. Strange as it may seem to outsiders, it's actually pretty simple for an alcoholic to find someone to fuck regularly. And while life for the alcoholic's sex partner is sure to be dynamic and unpredictable, knowing what to do is not always obvious. The owner at the rehab says you should do one thing. The overnight technician at the sober living house says to do another. The guy on tv contradicts both of them. Then, to make matters worse, you walk into a meeting designed to help someone in your very spot and the shares are so all over the place that you don't know whether to shit or go blind. What should be done by someone in your shoes? That's what this chapter shall aim to address. In the simplest way possible, we will attempt to offer helpful guidance to someone married to, shacking up with, or just plain banging, an alcoholic person.

Perhaps when you first met each other the drinking and drug use was sexy. After all, there's something quite romantic about being emotionally ignored and constantly lied to. At least at first. In the early days they looked good smoking a cigarette in some random bathroom, whilst spinning some new yarn of bullshit and staring at you with four-letter eyes. The two of you would knock it out one more time and then - boom - they'd be out the front door for a work function. Or for a week. Or for a month. You never really knew. You adjusted to being treated like a piece of shit because you were gonna fix this person. Sure, you'd never been able to work such a wonder in any of your earlier attempts to fix someone - not with a parent, nor with an ex. But this time you'd succeed. This was to be the long-awaited moment you were destined to swoop in and save someone from being unable to exhibit so much as an ounce of character.

As their drinking progressed, so did the speed at which you made unhealthy adjustments. You didn't notice, as it was like watching grass grow in reverse, but eventually, you'd lowered your standards and expectations to virtually nothing.

It may be helpful to first classify your sex partner specifically, as then the right approach will be plain to see. Your situation usually falls into one of four catagories.

One: your sex partner is an alcoholic. You can find their heart pretty easily, even though, particularly when they drink, they are capable of being complete and total fucking assholes.

Two: your sex partner smokes pot. They become less and less motivated. They don't do much, and what they do, they don't do that well. Trying to talk to them, you eventually come to realize that their brain is basically a setting sun.

Three: your sex partner does harder drugs - heroin, meth, and stuff like that. They look like an empty balloon, that is, if balloons were filled with souls. You really don't know who they are, and everything is scary now. You trust in the existence of elves more than you trust them.

Four: your sex partner huffs cleaning supplies. This is

just a straight psycho. Even in the pitch-black culture of the drug world, this person is a fucking weirdo.

Let's talk about the first three types, as those people should be dealt with in the exact same manner. The best thing to do is this: baby them. Baby the shit out of them. Keep them happy, as best you can. Consider it your full-time job to provide them with a pot for them to piss in, since they likely no longer have one. If you are a parent, did your child ever have a bicycle? Do you remember when they rode it without training wheels for the very first time? Do you recall running alongside the bicycle, making sure they didn't fall over or crash. Well you're doing the same thing here, except the child is twenty years old. Or thirty. Or forty. While running alongside a full-blown adult on an actual bike would be fucking weird, don't consider it to be in this case. Here it does them a tremendous service. They learn about their own capabilities when one removes all of their obstacles.

You might be tempted to follow your gut instinct and stop doing this kind of thing. If they tell you not to stop helping them, don't. They are healthy enough to call the shots. Besides, even if they are not, you just don't want anything bad to happen. It's no different than lighting off fireworks inside of your house so as not to inflict harm on any neighbors.

Let's go back to the sex partner described in the fourth catagory. The huffer.

I mean. *What the fuck* are you doing staying around them.

Sigh. Let's proceed.

Suppose now that your partner has gone into treatment, or a sober living house. A healthy mentality for you here is this: please just fix them and send them back to me better than ever. Usually that's how it goes with such places. They just make them all better and send them right back to your doorstep ninety days later wrapped in a ribbon. It is not necessary for you to make any adjustments while they are away. They were the entire problem. Spend some time distracting them while they are there, and definitely send conflicting messages as much as possible: "Stay there," "Come home," "Stay there." That sort of thing. And basically just get ready to resume life together in a way that is better than it ever was before.

Perhaps you don't have insurance, or you just have the regular amount of money most human beings have, and treatment is not an option. Your partner has thus decided to explore a 12-Step program. You may privately feel that free help based on ancient spiritual principles isn't worth two shits. Nevertheless, your partner regularly attends meetings and is now showing improvement. After about a month, force yourself to forget all the damage done to you by your partner's wanton and immoral behavior. Give them the keys back, if you will. If they'd been thrown out, let them move back in. Trust them with the cars and the kids. If they've stayed away from liquor and fentanyl for over thirty days, there's simply nothing to worry about anymore. If you're the enabler, shower them with money and pay their bills for them. This will help them become motivated to improve themselves.

Don't spy on them in any way because, as they'll be all too eager to remind you, that would only mean you're being bossy and controlling again. Just let them do whatever they please - to a point. If they start really getting into the whole 12-Step meeting thing, dissuade them. Tell them you'll leave them again unless they resume their old life - employment and all - immediately. None of that higher power shit if it's going to mean you'll have to work two jobs or wash more dishes. You just need a quick fix for the entire situation, and that's a rational way to look at it. It's easy to flip years of stuff around in a couple weeks or months.

Let's say, however, that your partner wants to keep on with all the 12-Step stuff. It all feels good to them, and their heart's actually opening up to a brand-new world that brims with compassion, support, and authentic comradery. They have hope for the first time. Fuck that. There's nothing there for you to learn more about or support. Dig in your heels and hold your ground. This approach is as good for you as it is for them. Let your disappointment simmer silently until it boils over into loud, close-to-constant, outright hostility. In such an atmosphere, what usually happens is the partner will just sorta snap out of it, and your troubles will fade away, and you'll start getting along better than ever. If any of this doesn't work out though, there's one more very popular option.

CHAPTER 9
IN REHAB AFTERWARD

Most people in rehab possess little to no sincere desire to be there. They're only there because they feel they've been bullied into it somehow, either by a person, by people, or by life. Perhaps a parent or a fuck-buddy has threatened to quit paying the bills for them. Or maybe they found themselves half naked and half blind on whiskey in a church parking lot and a cop showed up at the wrong time, and now there's this annoying thing with the court. Or perhaps things were just getting too complicated in the outside world and the rehab-lifestyle of warm beds and hot meals started to look downright appealing, particularly if your insurance company, or literally anyone else for that matter, was willing to foot the bill. Regardless of the circumstances leading up to it, you're in rehab now and what are you going to do? It is with this chapter that we aim to answer that question fully, in detail, so you can get the most out of your stint in virtually any treatment facility.

Some new residents make the mistake of listening to what staff members, counselors and various clinicians have to say about recovery. Don't do this. It is you who should be explaining recovery to them, and to anyone who will listen for that matter. This includes fellow residents. Moments after you've strewn your shit all over the floor in your new living quarters, bum a smoke from someone and tell everybody living there what's up. While this is a mindset you'll want to keep throughout your stay, there are also some other things you'd be wise to start focusing on immediately. First, what are the "proper responses" to questions posed to you by staff? In other words, *what do they want to hear*? Accurately determining this, and responding accordingly, is important because it really serves your best interests in the long run. Effectively achieving this shall require steadfast observation on your part that is at once subtle and yet acute. Remember, your objective in rehab is threefold: maintain your social standing as a total bullshit artist, present yourself as an expert on recovery, and get the reality you've created on the outside world to fuck right off.

If you don't feel a sexual commitment to anyone in your life, be on the lookout for people you might be able to fuck. Start by flirting with anyone remotely attractive; these are desperate times. Don't get depressed if the pickins seem slim at first. Brand new residents with lots of luggage but little boundaries will be stumbling through the entrance on a regular basis. Keeping yourself occupied with this type of shit is not only excellent for your own recovery, it's genuinely loving to your slowly dying fellow residents.

If you are in a facility that uses the 12-Step model, be the verbal equivalent of someone pulling down their pants, and squatting, and just shitting all over all of it. Don't allow a positive thing to be said about the 12-Steps or that lifestyle in your presence. If anyone there is getting something out of a 12-Step program, be a relentless storm with thunder and lightning and dump torrential rain on their parade. Whenever you find yourself doing this, pat yourself on the back and know that you are not only acting as a force of good in the world, but you're also ensuring that your stay in treatment facilities will likely be brief.

Some rehabs insist you go to meetings regardless of your feelings about them. Once faking sick runs its course, do go along, but drag your feet. Make the van's restless cluster of passengers wait for you for seemingly hours as you stagger about the facility grounds frantically searching for a lighter or one of your missing flip-flops.

Once at the meeting, spend most of your time outside, socializing - but not about recovery. Look for other people who don't give a shit about any of it and bond with them. Note that your dating pool just got bigger. Look around for people of easy virtue. If you have a cellphone, get numbers of people you might be able to have some sort of sex with later on. If you're not really into anyone there then spend your time in the parking lot either bashing recovery or bragging about something. This is a landscape where you're sure to have steep competition, so be prepared to talk over all the other braggarts.

Let's now say that you are in a rehab that has you seeing a therapist and attending groups. The same principles we discussed regarding 12-Step meetings should be applied. However, in this setting you should go through the motions way more. In other words, say the right thing more frequently. Not because you mean it, but because you don't want to get thrown out. There are scared loved ones who are hoping you take this seriously, so honor them a tiny bit by at least doing the bear minimum. It's usually simple to manipulate this system. Not always, but often. So just do the best you can, and attempt to get even better at manipulation, as you will need this skill at your next facility.

It may seem as if there's a lot for you to do, but there's not. Spend most of your time complaining, or doing literally nothing. Gripe about anything you can think of - the way the place is run, the food, the staff - you name it. Do your part to prevent any positive energy from ever infiltrating the place. If you tend to mope or isolate, turn it up. Stay in your room. Mindlessly watch tv for hours on end. Be the person who lies on the couch all day gazing at your phone, barely flinching until the next house obligation inevitably taps your shoulder.

Some odds and ends. Should anyone bring up medication, remember you're an expert on that too. So sound off about those things, as well. Don't act like you do not have a medical license simply because you don't have a driver's license. If you're required to do chores of any kind, do them only when forced to do so, and tell everyone you're an adult who should not have to be told what to do. An ongoing and loud expression of such sentiments will often rile up fellow housemates, garnering you more respect amongst those not interested in ever getting the fuck out of such places.

An entire book could be written about the many dimensions of being in rehab. But what we've supplied you with is more than enough to set you on the right track. Use these suggestions as a rough outline of how you should behave. And above all else, don't try to actually improve yourself while you are there. That would only increase your chances of a way, way shorter stay.

CHAPTER 10
A VISION ASKEW

We don't really know what drinking means for most normal folks. All we know is that the last days of our drinking flat-out *sucked*. We could go on, but, as you have heard countless times by now, we never really had a drinking problem. We have a thinking problem, totally unrelated to alcohol. And no matter how long we abstain from drinking, this will always be true. Our real issues are many: we have bad pickers, we're "more whores", we have "great forgetters", we are compulsive, we are in denial, and even with long-term sobriety, we are still outright mental defectives, unable to ever trust our own thinking.

Every once in a while a newcomer says, "Wow, I feel better. Something's happening, but I can't explain it. I actually have hope!" As alcoholics still making things about us, we smile at such a fool. We know that sensation - the pink cloud - and we know it will soon evaporate into faint, forever-fading hues. Just wait until life starts to happen to this poor son-of-a-bitch. Soon it will be his turn in the barrel. He won't get paid enough at work. People will disagree with him. Relationships won't work out. People will cut him off on the freeway. Life will begin to annoy him as much as it annoys some of us. Then he will know stress like we do. He will wish he could just catch a fucking break for once. He will run like hell to the nearest noon meeting.

We have shown you what is common these days. You say,

"Yes, I'm willing. But am I to live a life where I shall be all stressed out and unhappy like so many others I see? I know I can't drink or shoot heroin anymore, but now what should I do? Do you have a substitute?"

Kinda. We have meetings we can cling to for an hour out of the day. And that's better than nothing. There you will find a place where you can hide from real life for a while. And even if you don't form any new relationships there, at least you'll be met by a crowd willing to sit there and listen to you battle people, places, and things.

Years ago, the physician who most greatly contributed to the original book published a statement about slips and human nature, illuminating just how far off the track we have strayed in terms of what is uniquely wrong with us as alcoholics. But by then, as a society, we had already taught ourselves far too much to compute what he was saying, or to even be bothered.

In recent years a growing number of people have concluded that meetings alone might not actually be enough to keep an alcoholic sober. Fortunately, there are hundreds of sober livings now, for just that reason. There we can lock ourselves away, thus avoiding temptation from drugs and alcohol until we have regained our own mental strength. Some will spend years in sober living, for they've come to believe they don't have what it takes to make it in the outside world. And scores never give themselves the opportunity to find out whether or not that's true. Since sober livings are without formal regulation of any kind, literally *anyone* can open one! Happily for everyone, this trend is already in full swing, thus assuring that the message of recovery will only become clearer and better over time.

Better news still: practically anyone can work in the treatment field after being dry for just a month or two. It's good for the sober house and it's great for the employee. Everyone knows people who work in this field are just a lot happier. They just freakin' glow. Moreover, these people no longer had to be help other alcoholics for free. Now they could also get a rapidly revolving door of new friends and three hots and a cot.

We know what you are thinking. You are saying to yourself, "None of this seems right. In fact, *this whole message feels way off.*" You forget you cannot trust your own thinking. You're just being defiant. To duplicate what we have described is only a matter of attending meetings.

Still you might say, "But what if the meetings near me suck?" We cannot be sure. So you must remember that your real reliance should always be on your sponsor. They will tell you which meetings are good, and which ones are shit.

Our book is meant to be humorous and thought-provoking. We realize we know very little. But we do know the original message was is about the very opposite of what you've just read. Ask Him what you can do each day to help everyone around you, because it's our only real job now. The answers will come, unless we are only thinking about ourselves. Obviously we cannot transmit much when we are only thinking about ourselves.

Abandon yourself to good if you don't understand God. Admit your faults, because we all have them. Clear away the wreckage you've created. Help other alcoholics in your spare time, and join us. We are right here with you in the fellowship, and you will surely meet more of us on this bumpy road you can call your own beautiful journey.

May God bless you - until then.

AFTERWARD

Before this book was published, I shared it with many of my friends in recovery. They roared with laughter. They sometimes cringed. Yet every one of them looked up at me many times while reading it to say, "Oh my God, this is so *true* though!"

I hope this book allows us to laugh at ourselves. I do not believe we arrived at this point on purpose; the most amazing people I have ever known make up our beloved fellowship, which I in no way wish to imply I represent in any way. I'm just one person.

Not everyone will understand that this book truly comes from love. I claim absolutely nothing special about myself, for I have seen my own inventories and know full-well I am in no position to judge another soul. But in my heart of hearts, I do sincerely hope this book provides people with laughs, and that it maybe even helps someone.

- *"Clay F."* (Feet of Clay)

Copyright 2020 H.J. F. Books // All Rights Reserved

Links to PODCAST and to all other books at:

sarcasticbigbook.com

THE NO STEPS PRAYER

Lord, make me a channel of confusion - that where there is hatred, I may stir the pot - that where there is wrong, I may point it out - that where there is harmony, I may bring discord - that where there is truth, I may bring lies - that where there is faith, I may bring doubt - that where there is light, I may cast shadows. Let me seek only to be comforted, understood, and loved - for it is by thinking about myself that I will find true peace, and answers to all the right questions

- "Clay F"

BOOKS BY THIS AUTHOR

Sarcastic Daily Meditations

A meditation on what is precisely what is untrue 365 days a year.

The First Two Columns Of A Fourth Step: 365 Daily Affirmations That Won't Help You One Bit

Read a ridiculous resentment each and every day that is sure to make you laugh at yourself as well as brighten your mood

Printed in Great Britain
by Amazon